Floral Bouquets

and Fantasy Butterflies

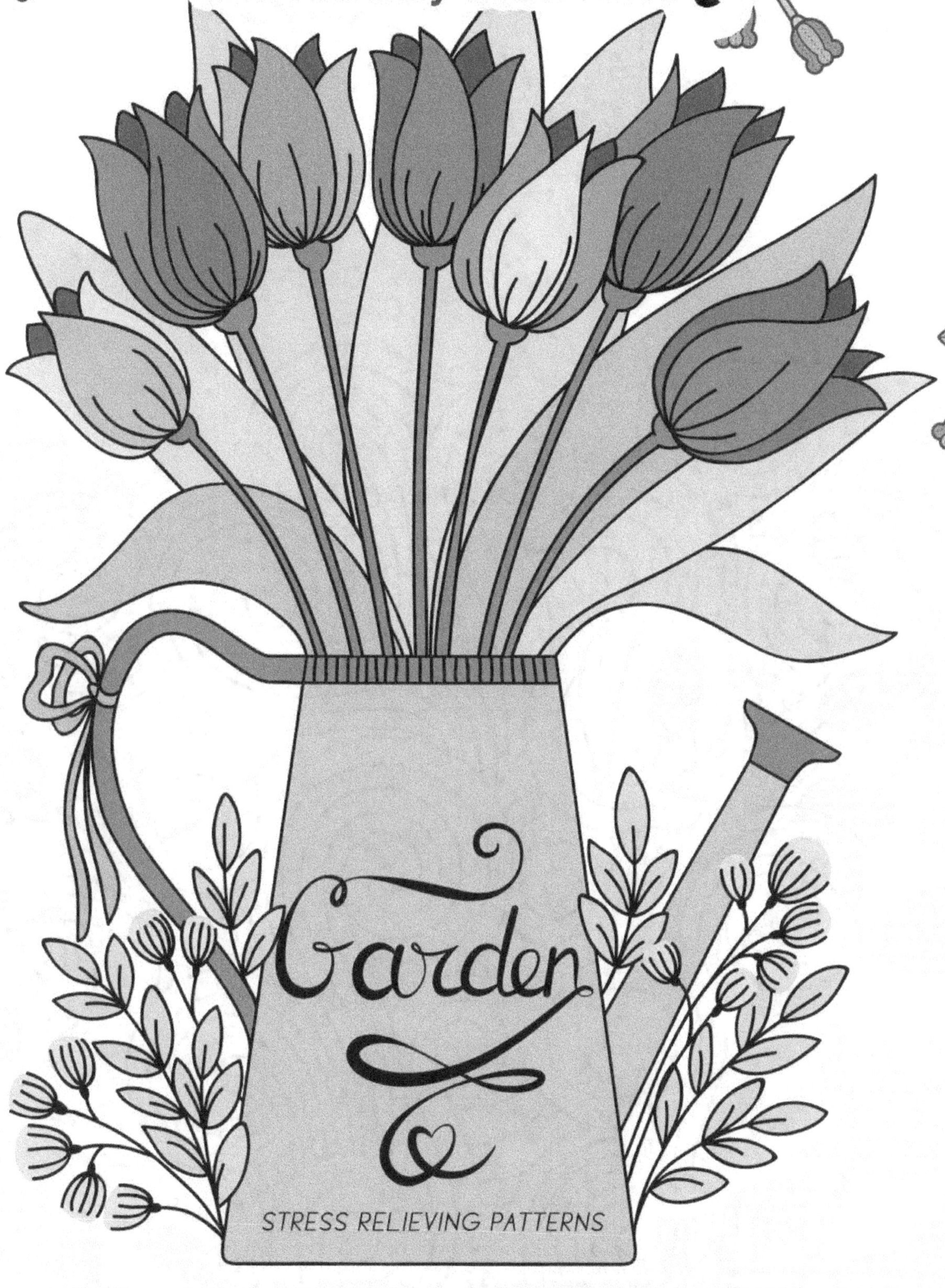

COLORING BOOKS FOR ADULTS

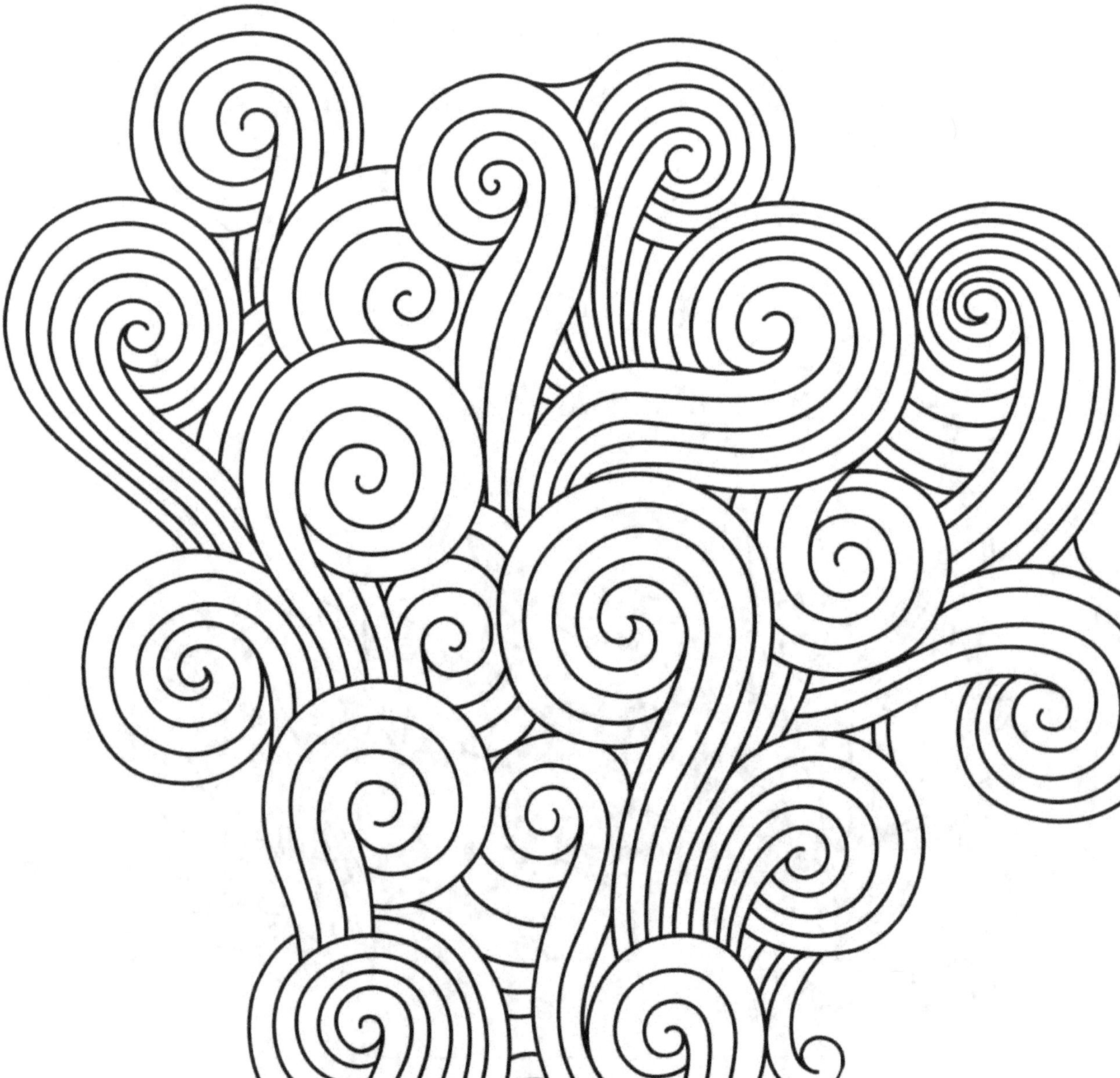

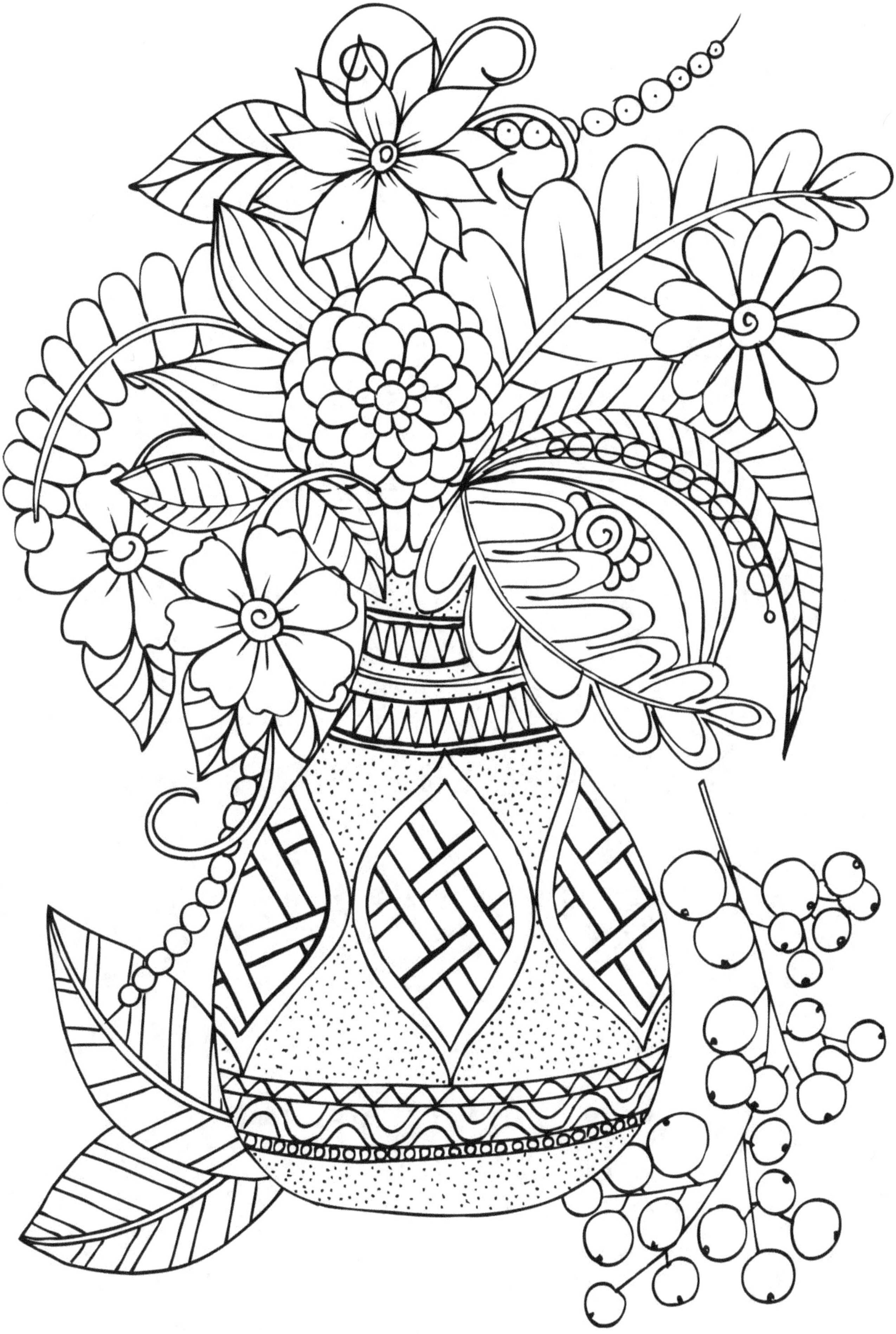

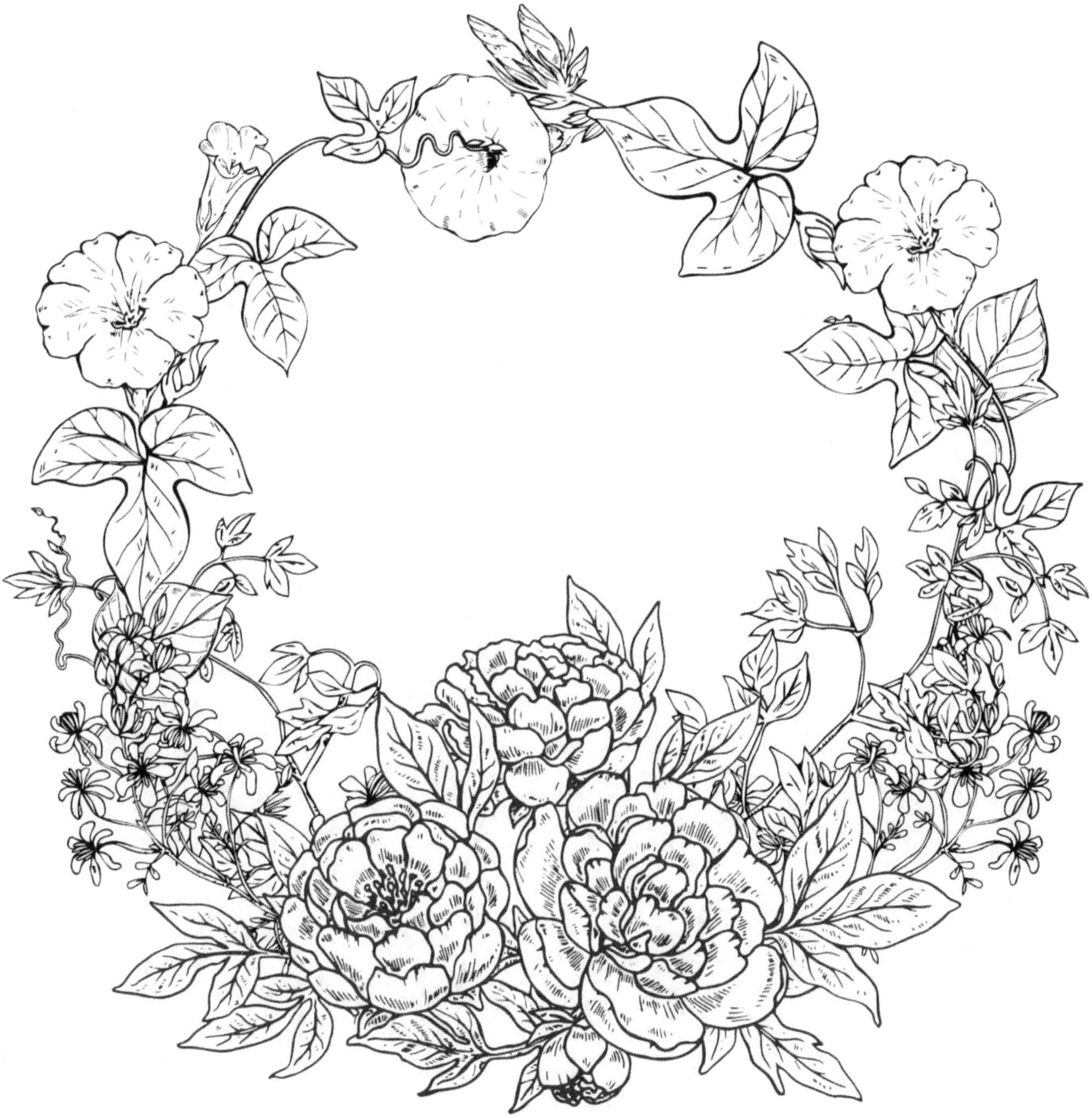

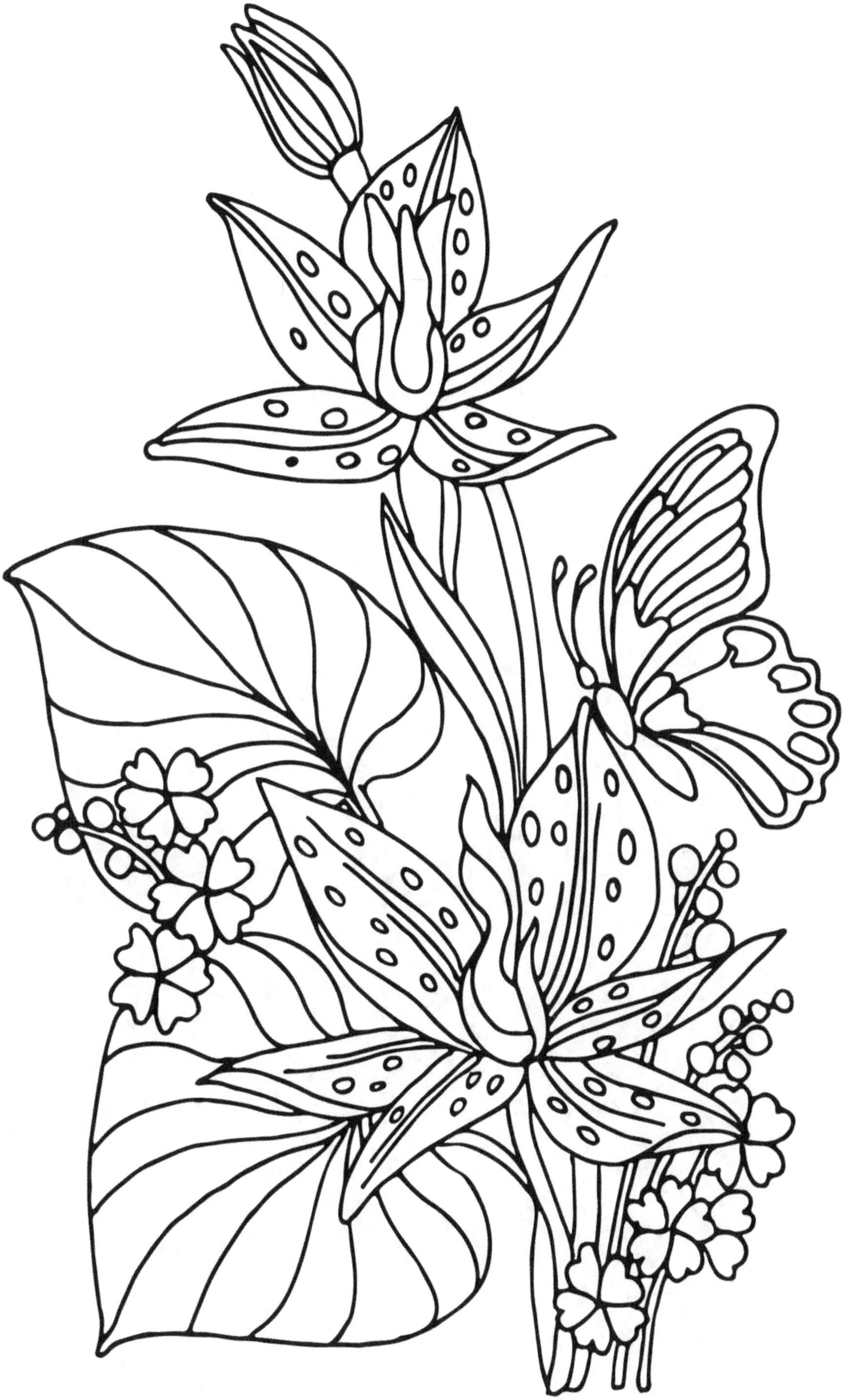

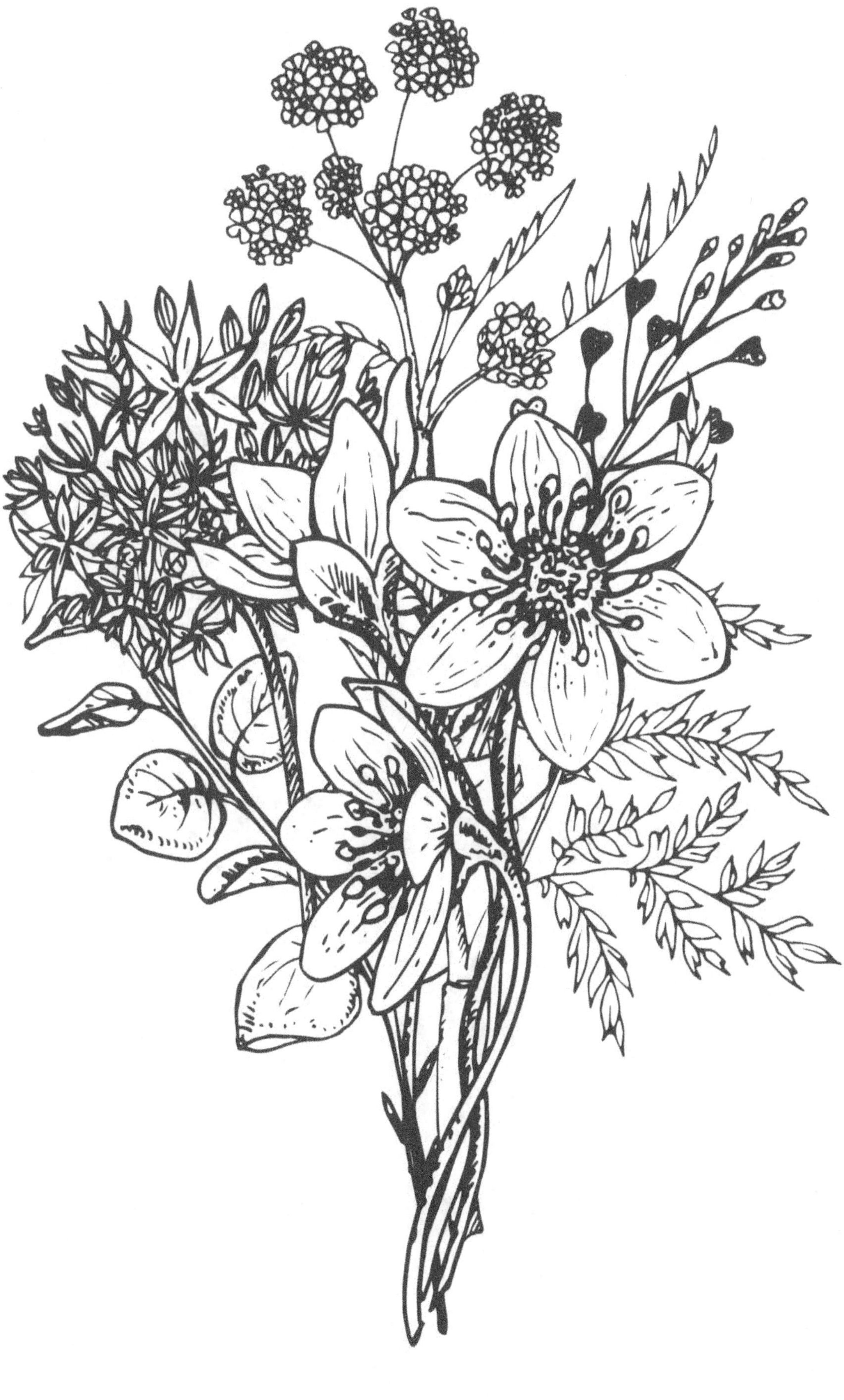

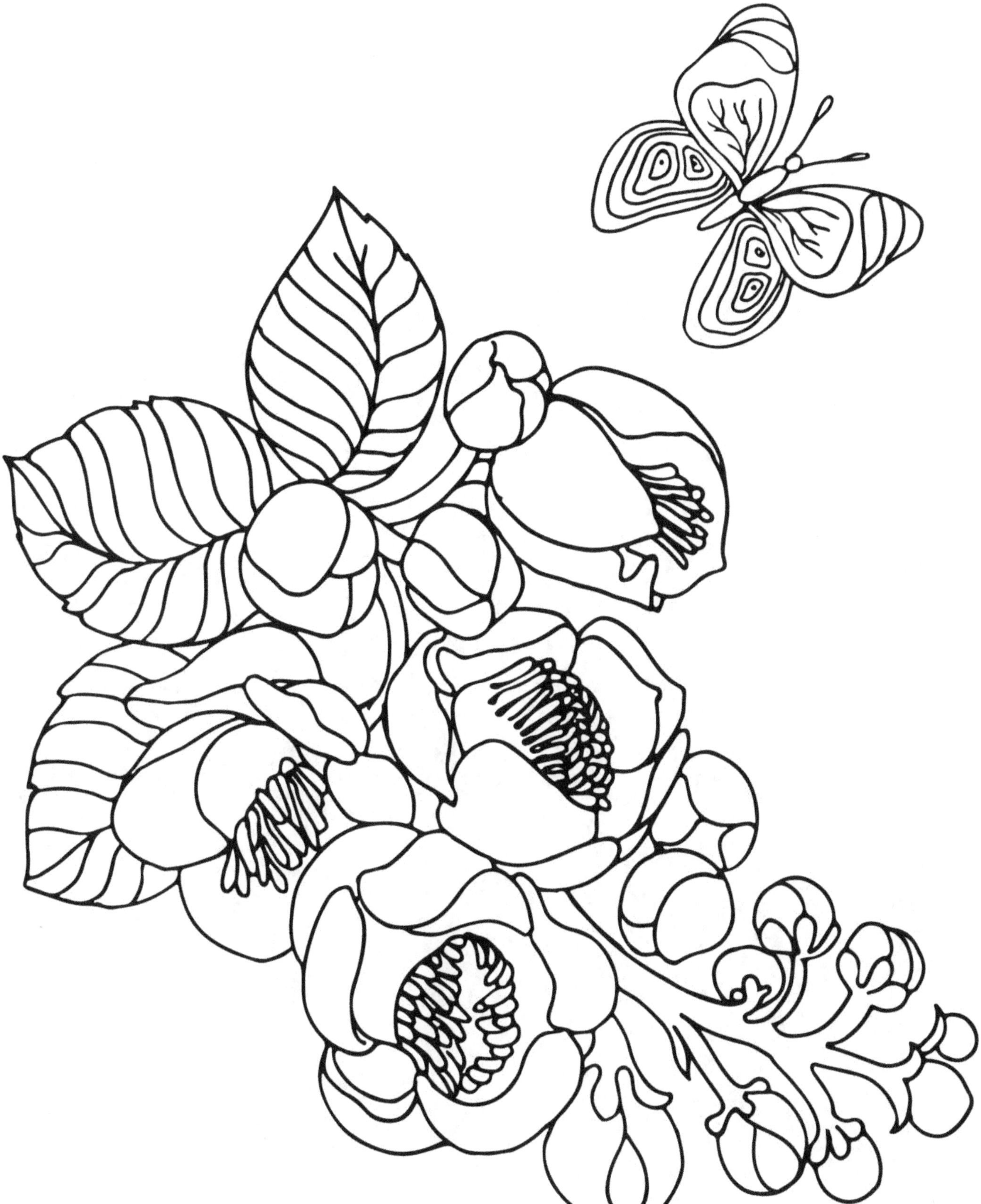

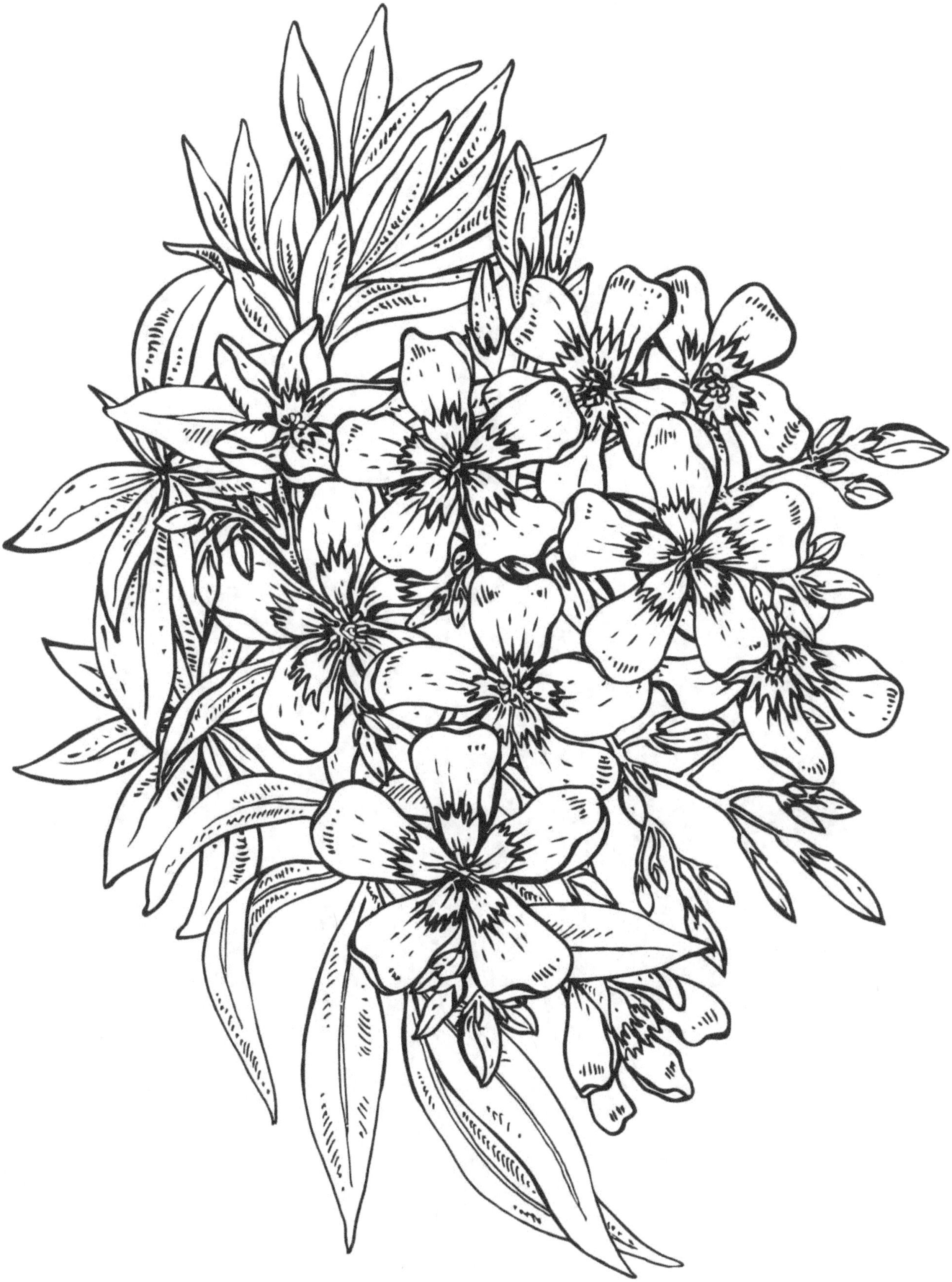

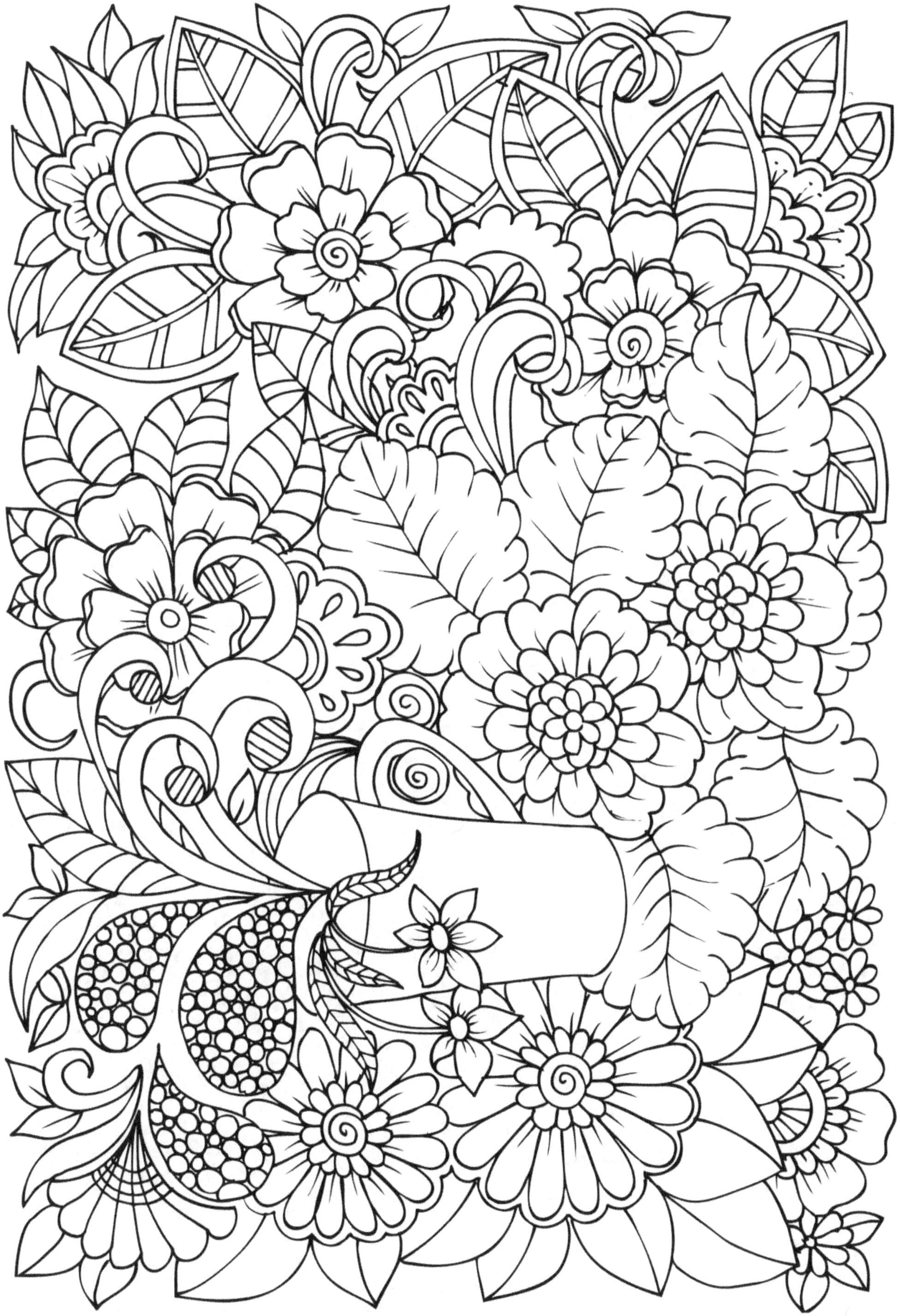

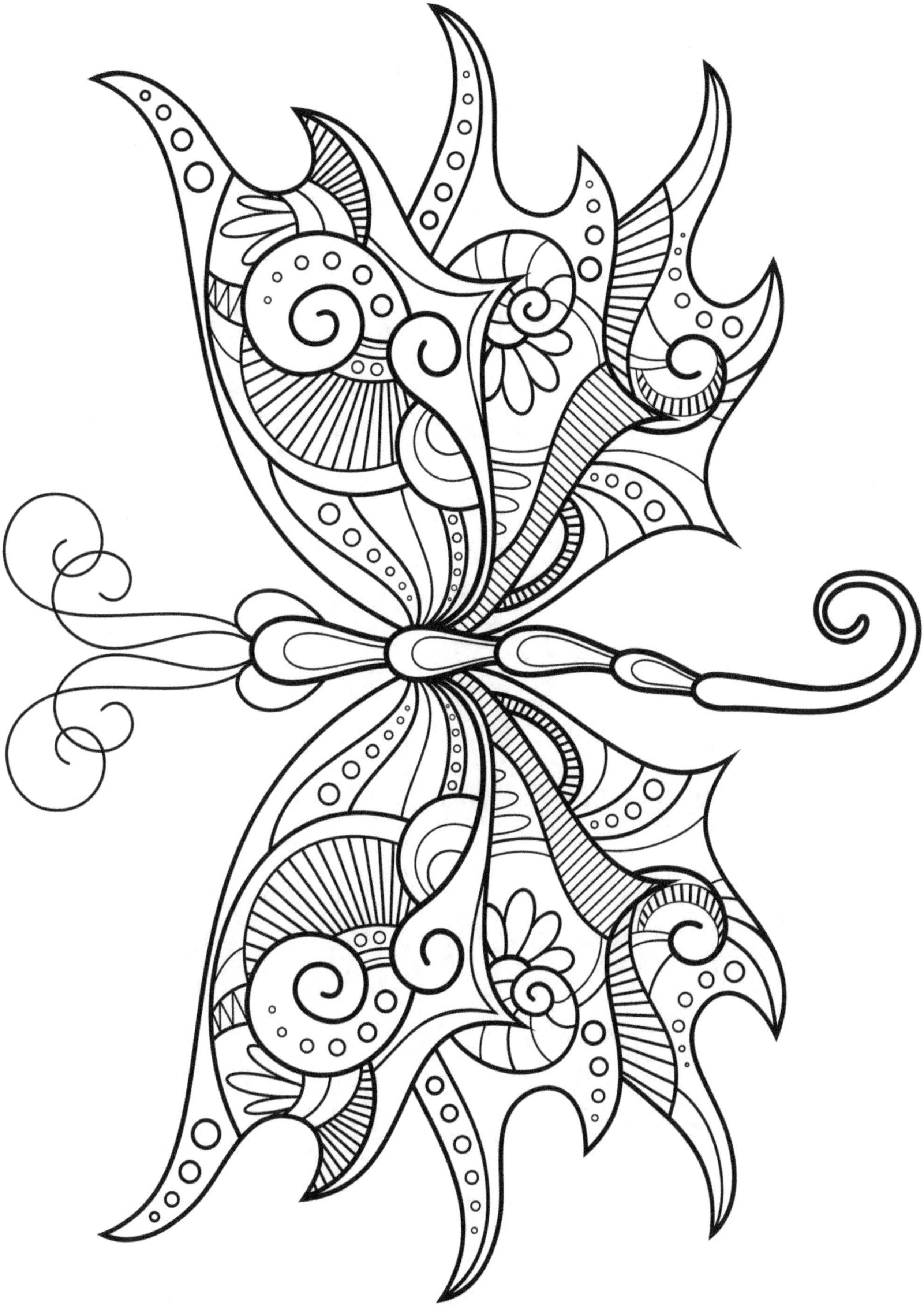

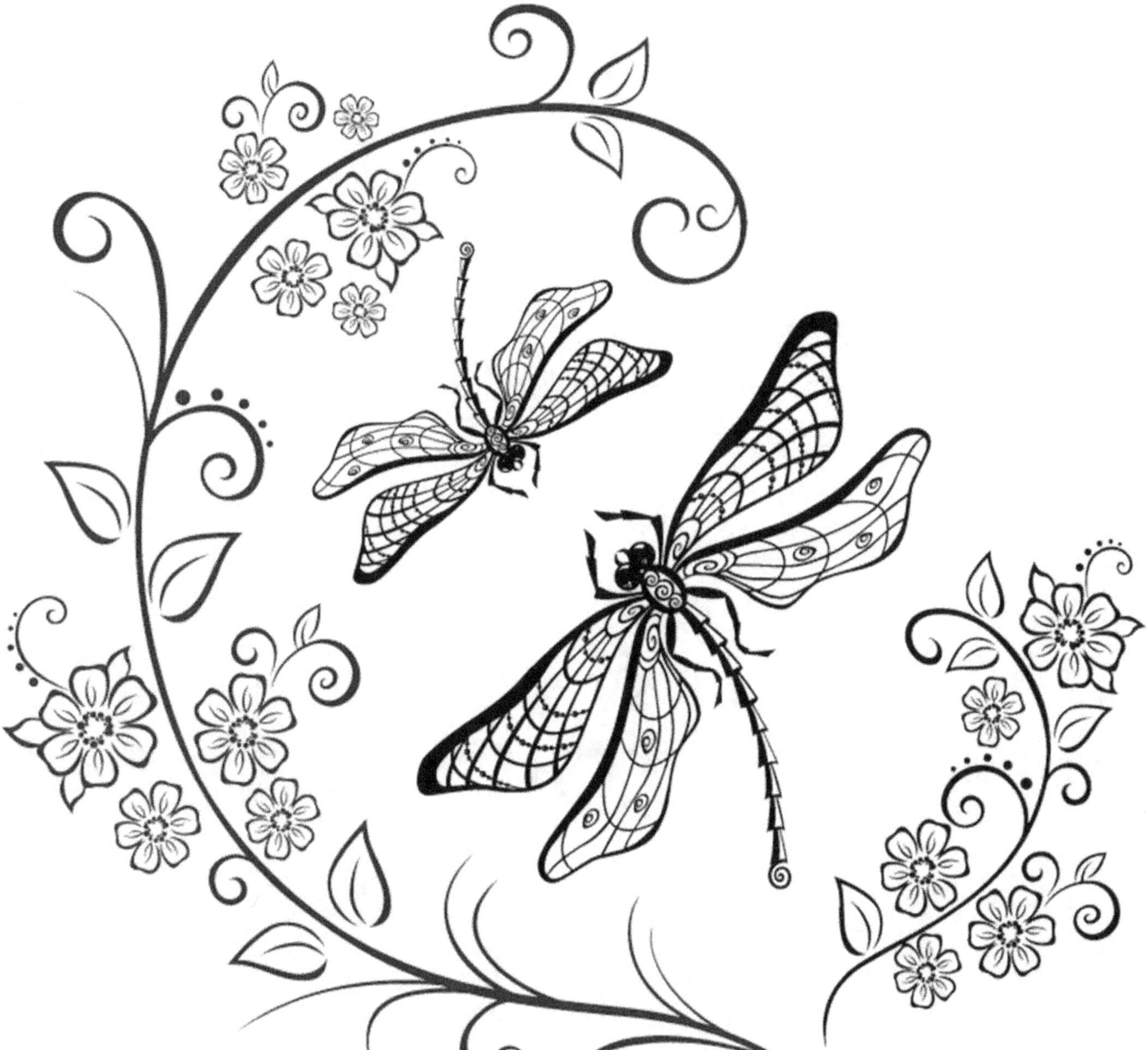

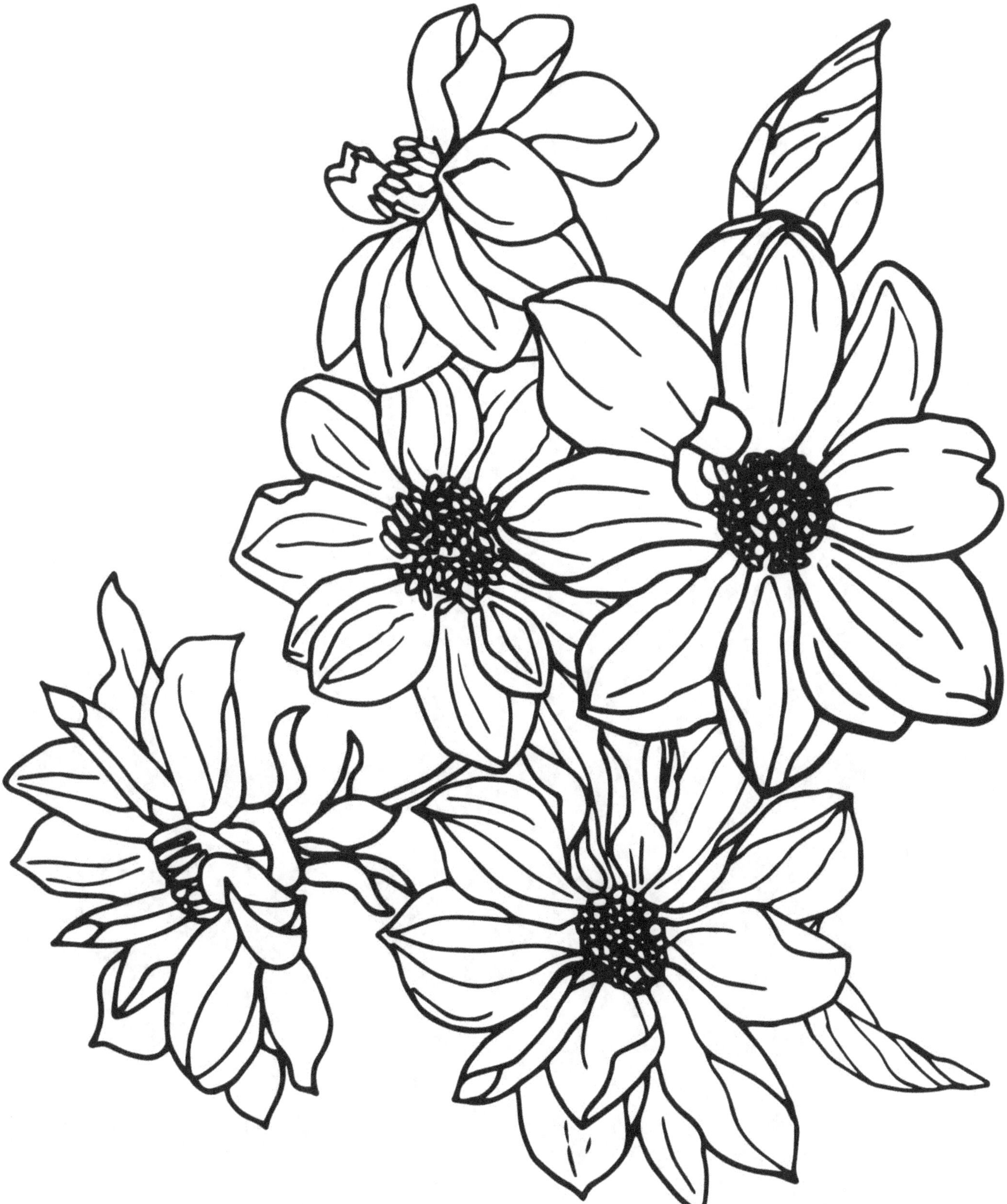

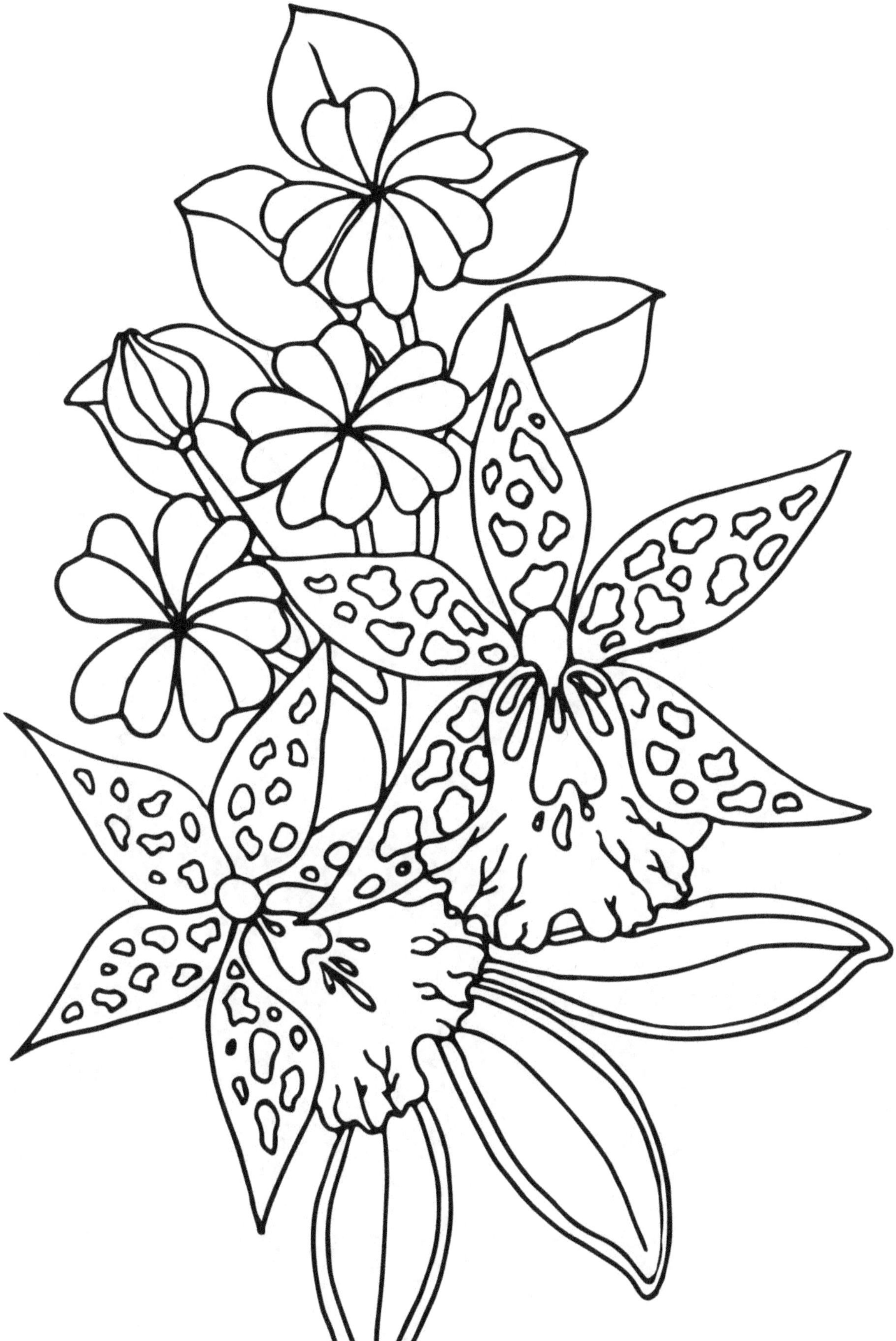

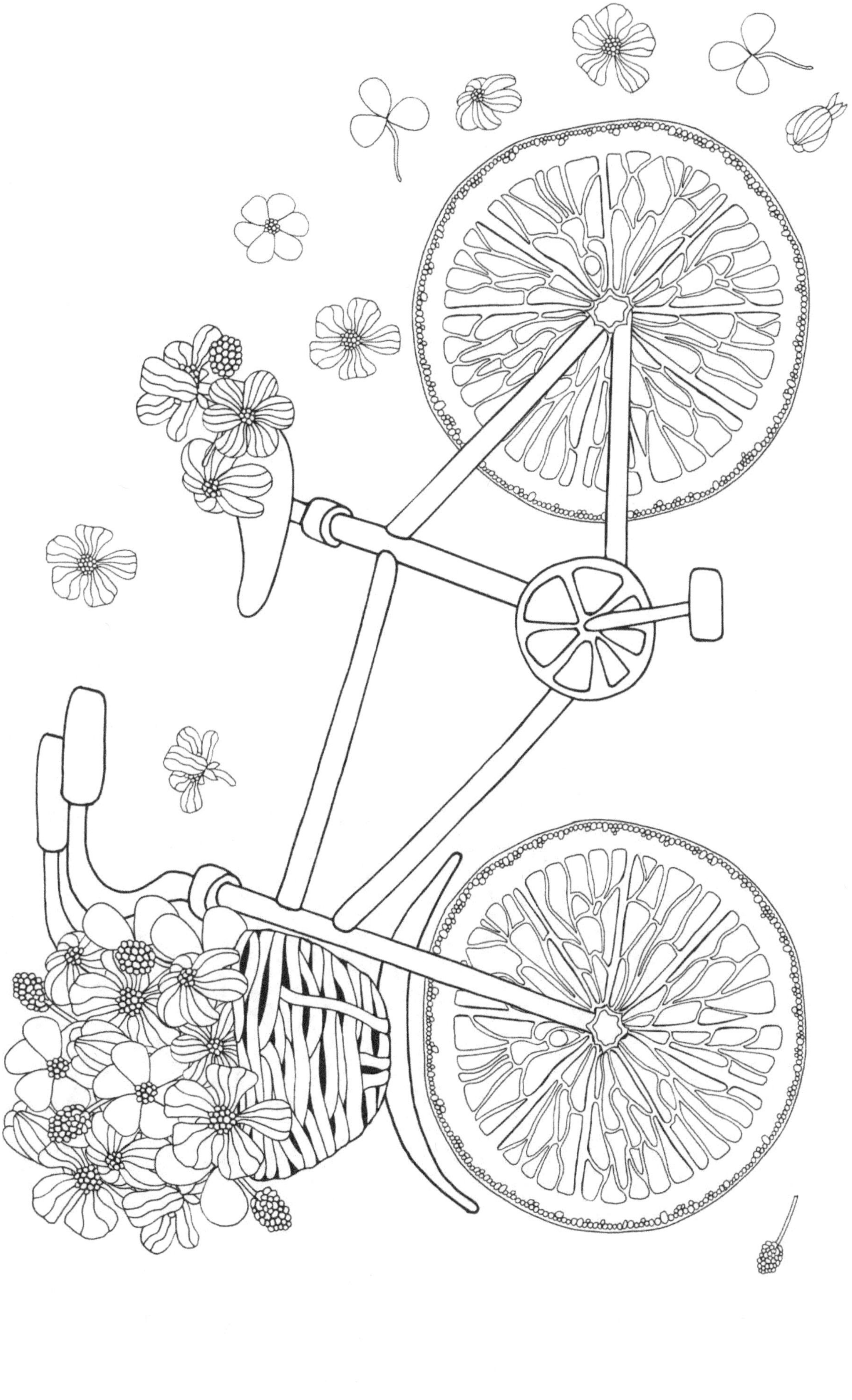

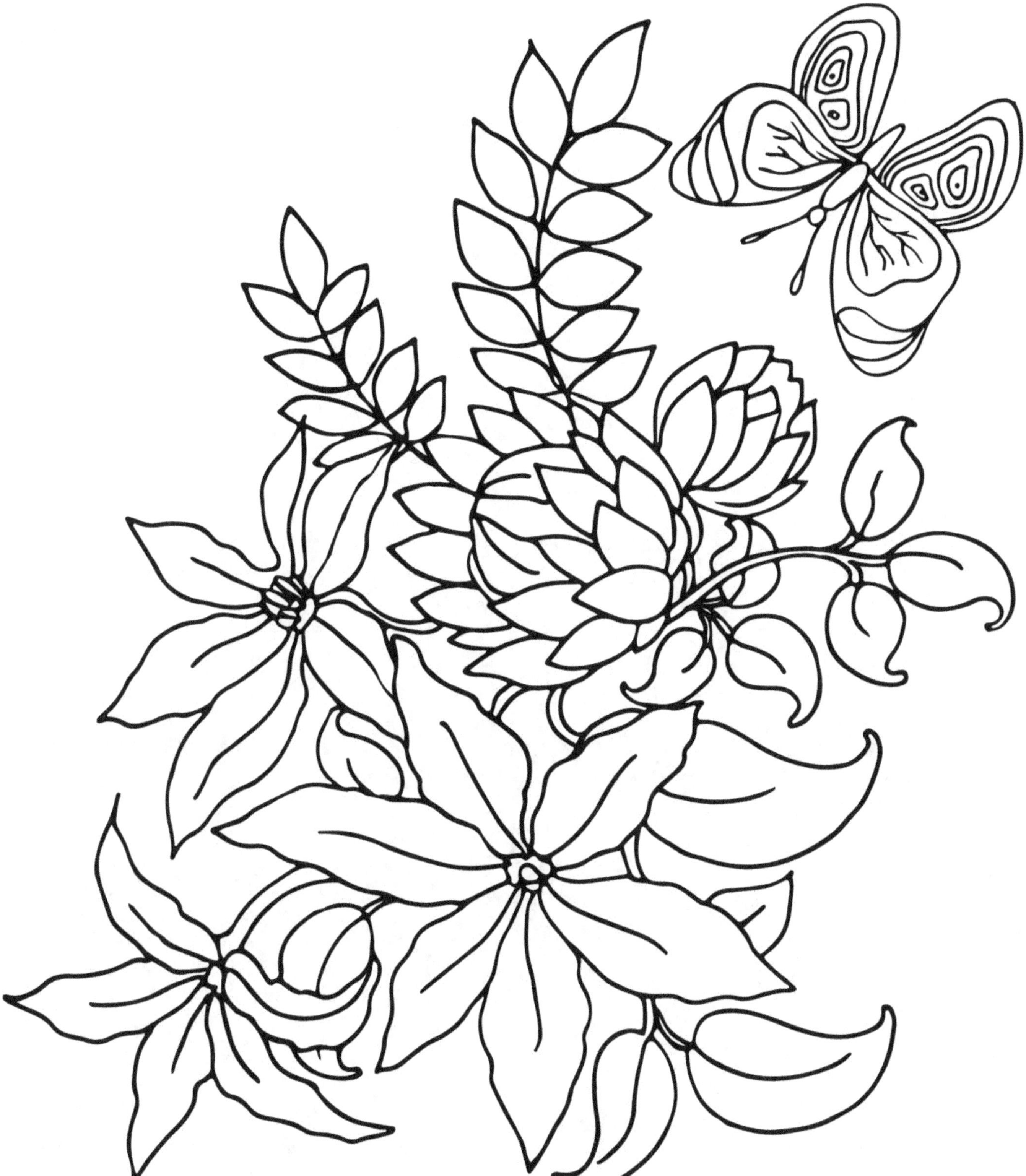

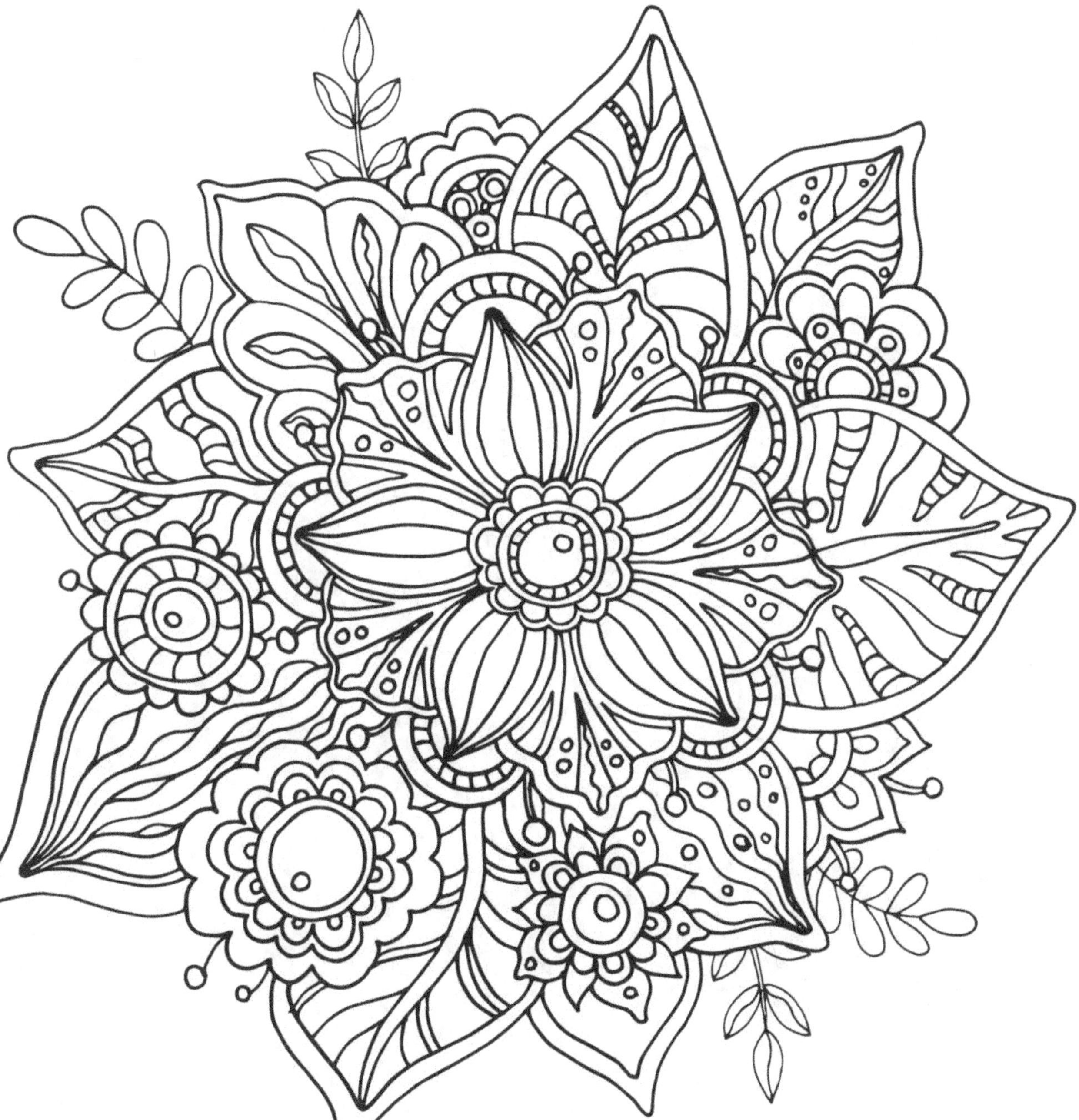

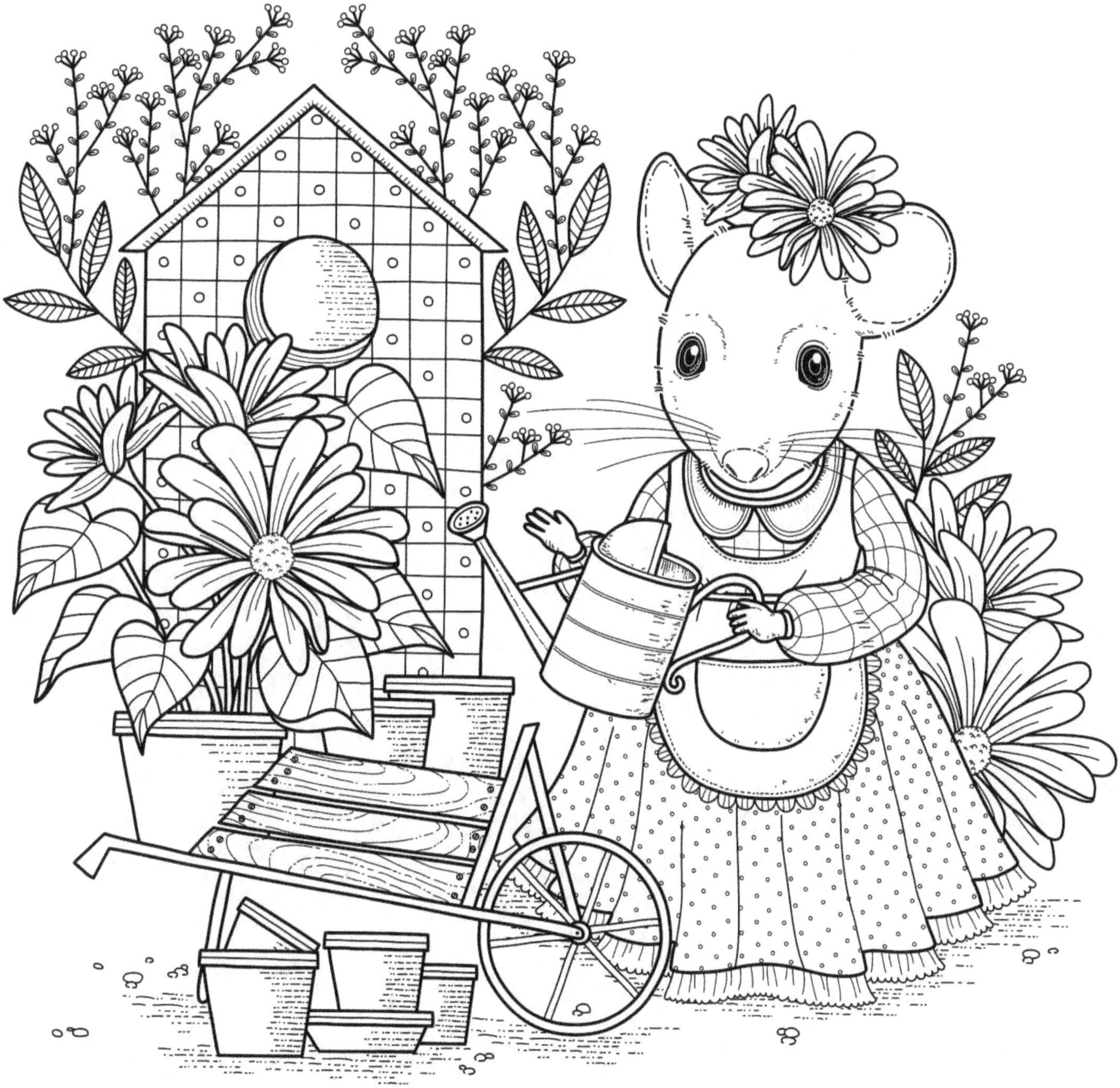

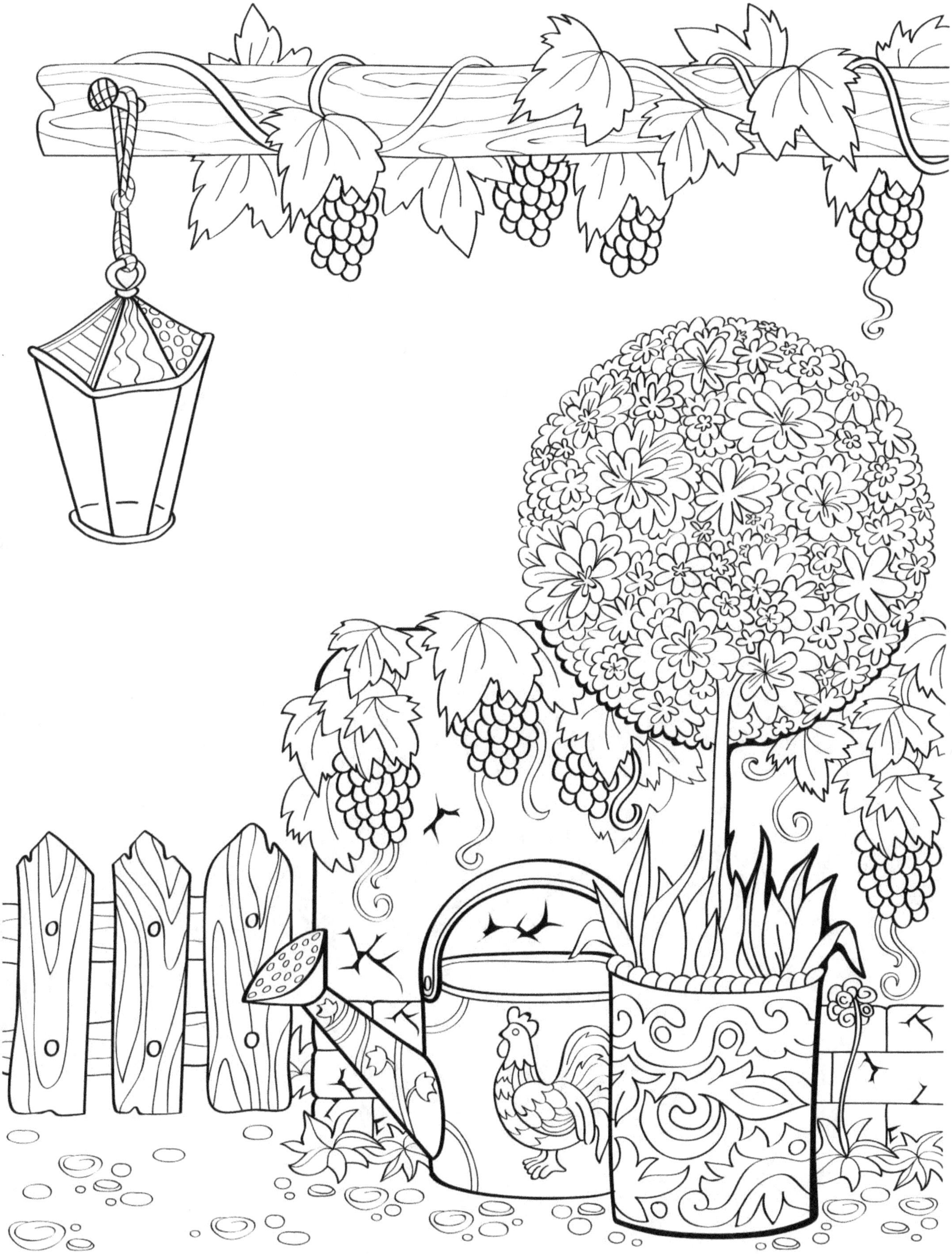

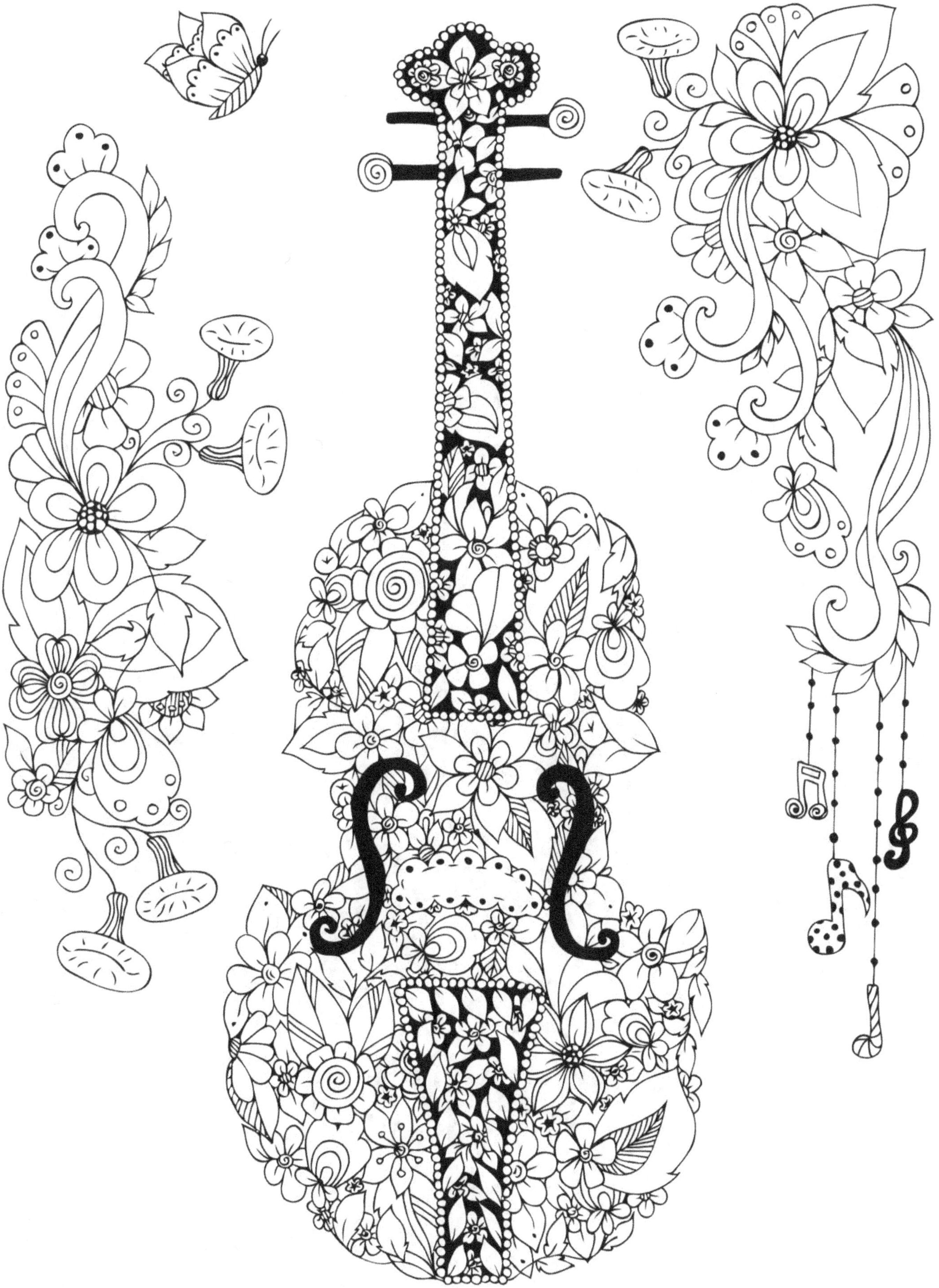

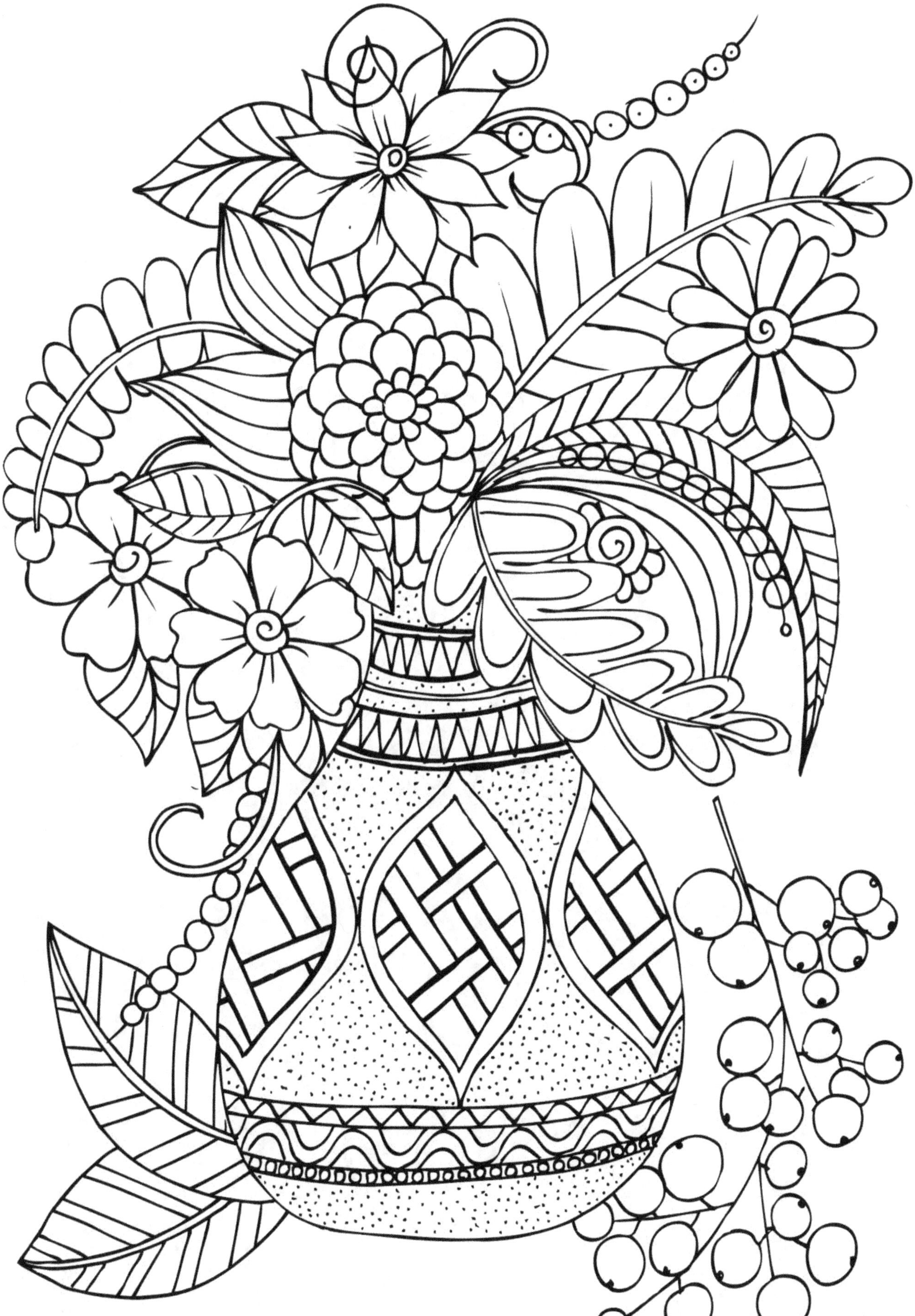

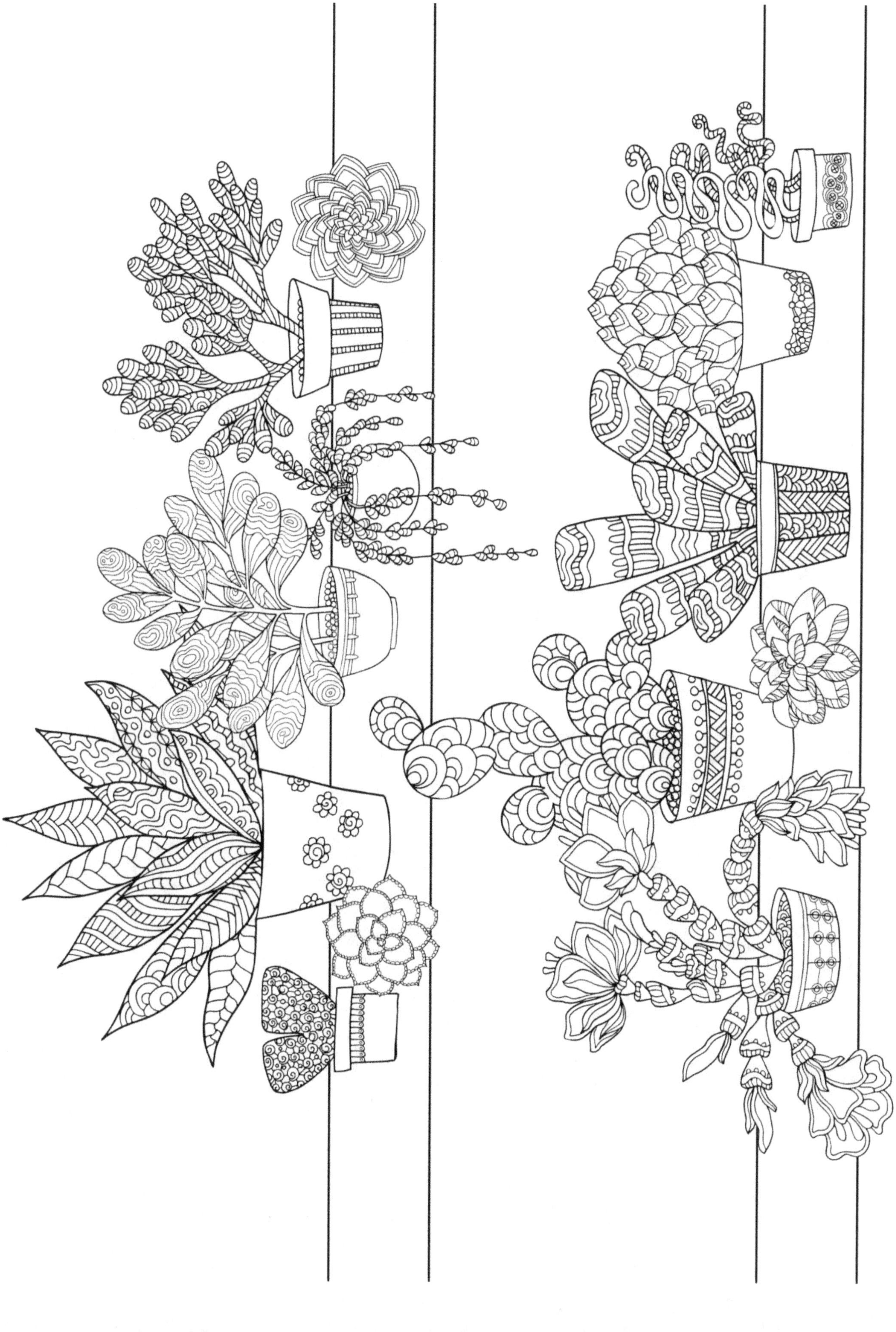

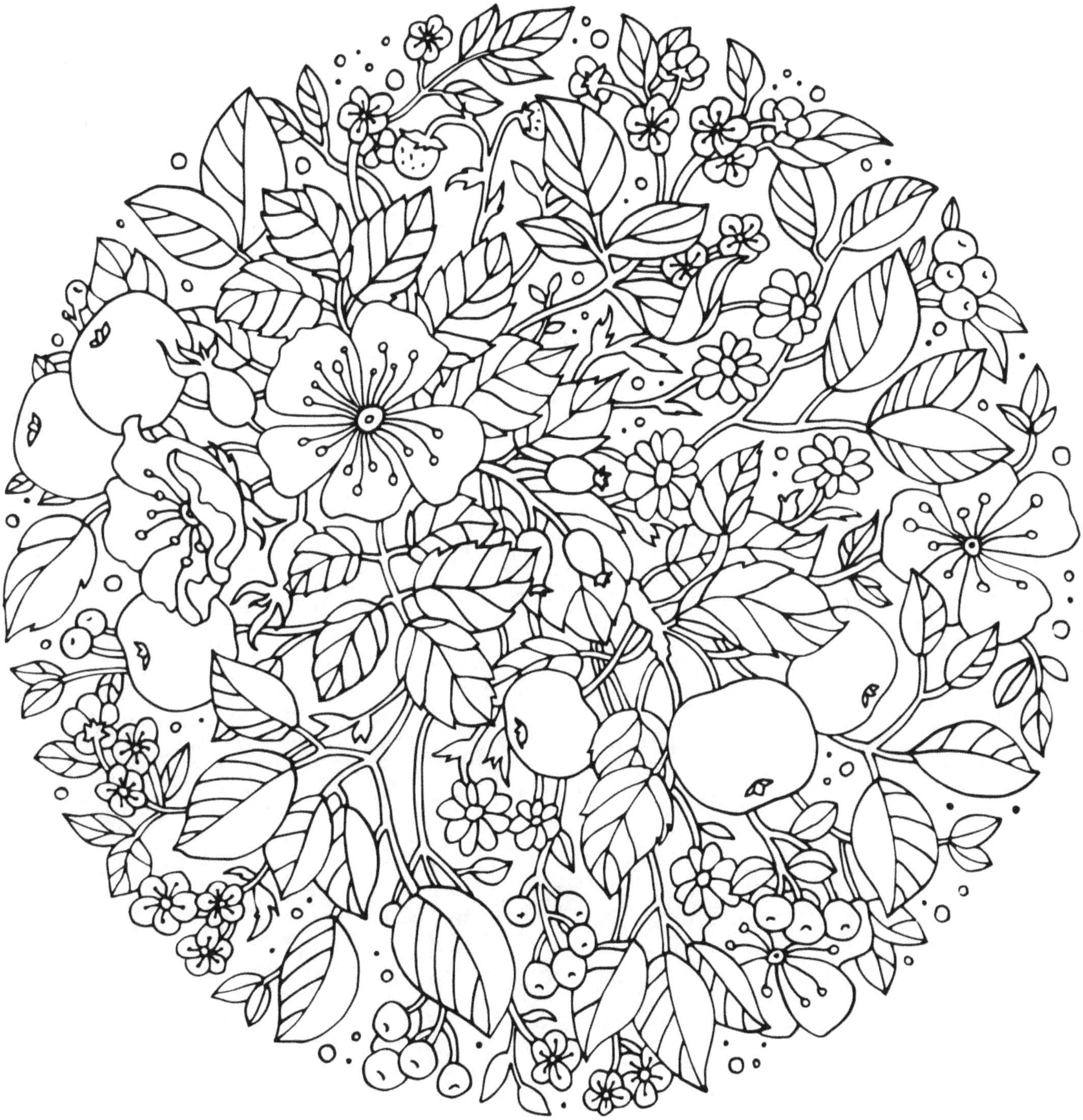

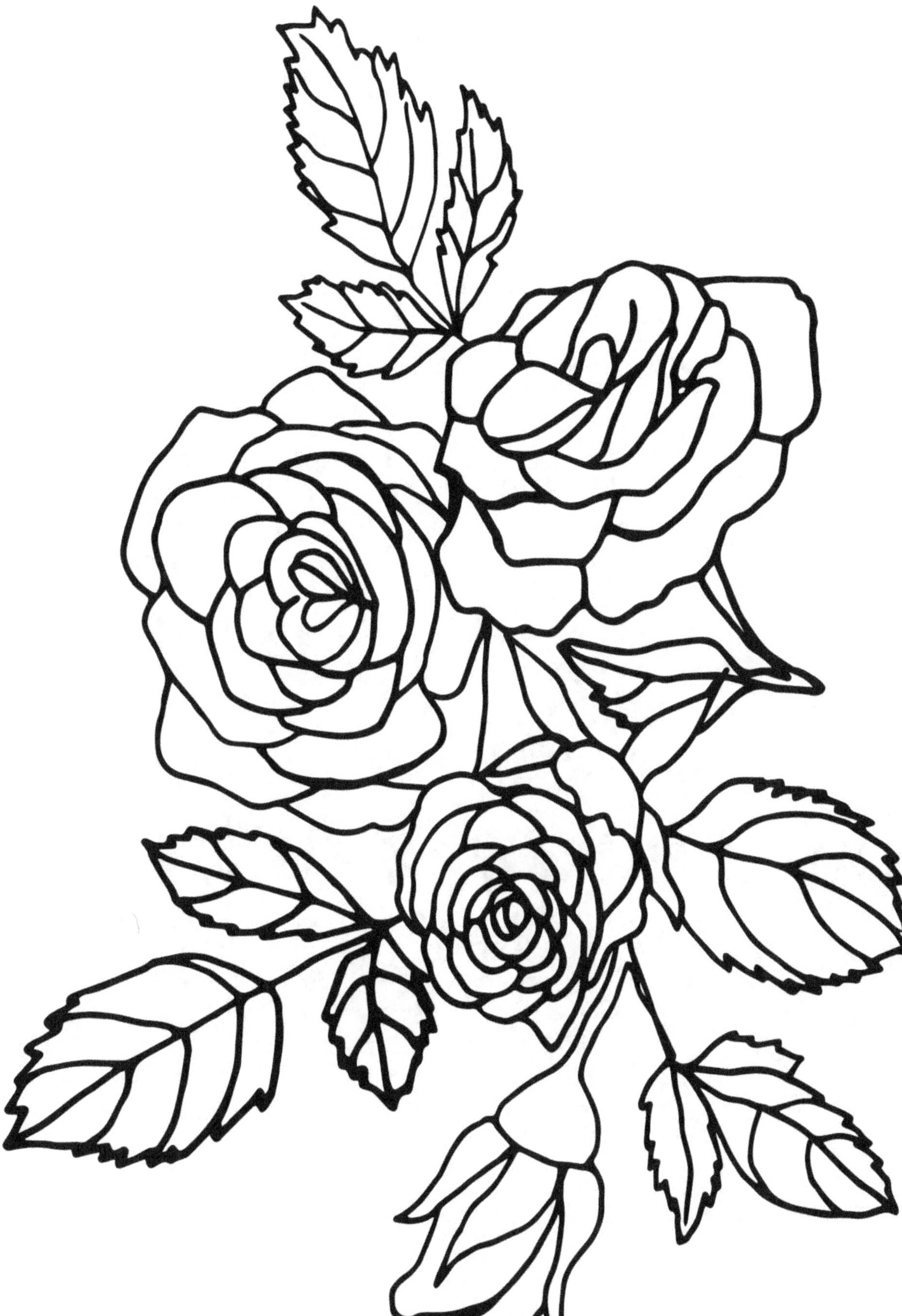

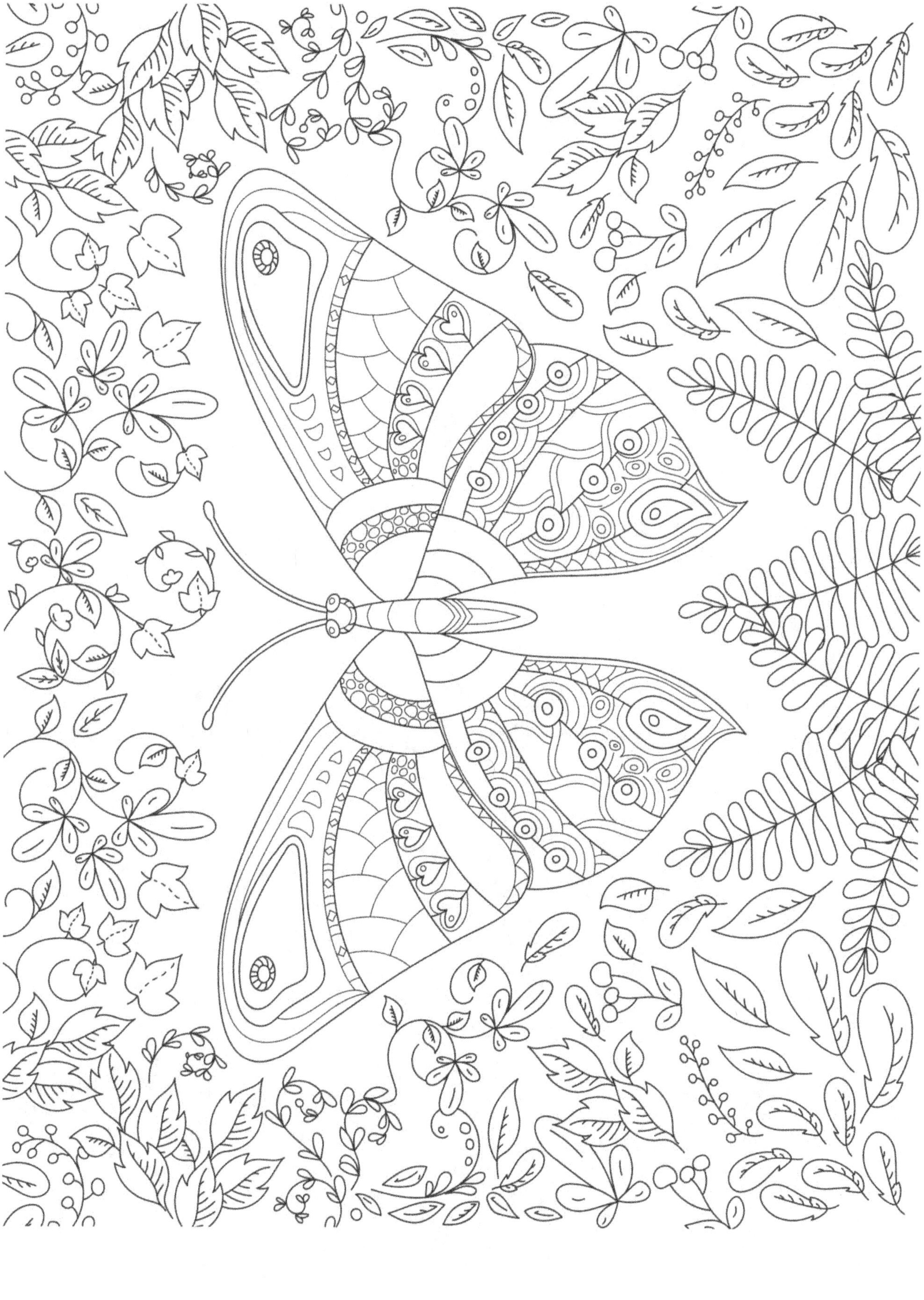

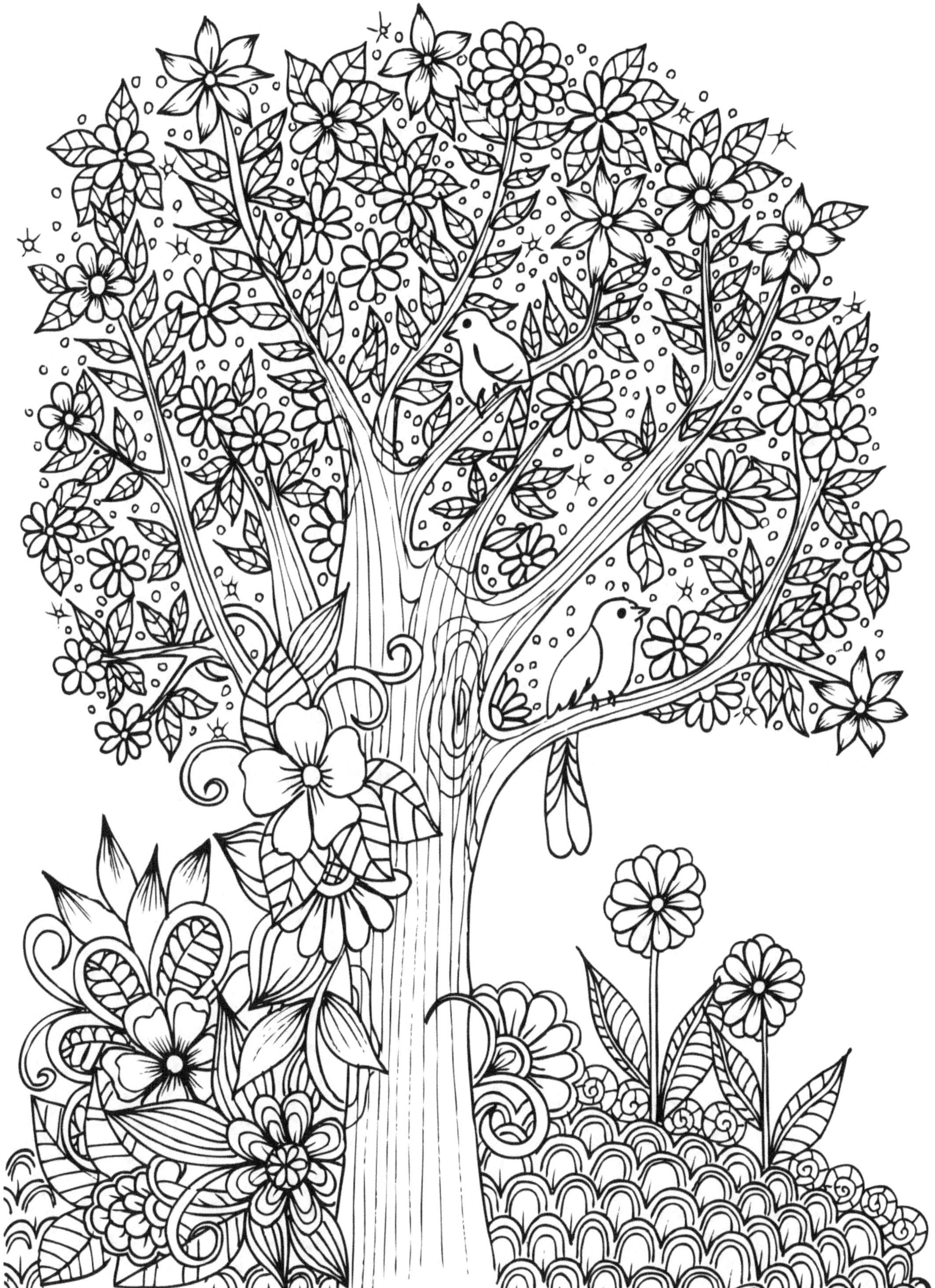

www.ingramcontent.com/pod-product-compliance
Lightning Source LLC
Chambersburg PA
CBHW081604280526
45788CB00011B/3545